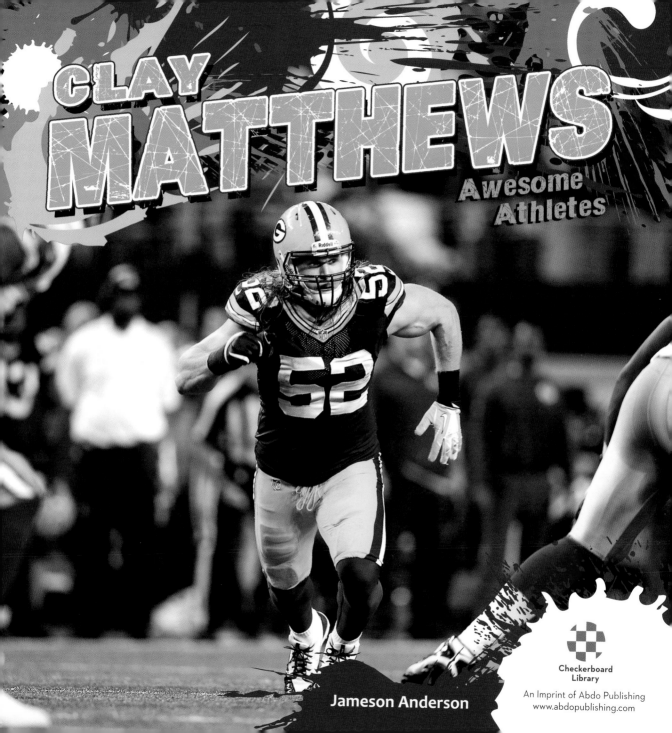

CLAY MATTHEWS

Awesome Athletes

Jameson Anderson

Checkerboard
Library

An Imprint of Abdo Publishing
www.abdopublishing.com

www.abdopublishing.com

Published by Abdo Publishing, a division of ABDO, PO Box 398166, Minneapolis, Minnesota 55439. Copyright © 2015 by Abdo Consulting Group, Inc. International copyrights reserved in all countries. No part of this book may be reproduced in any form without written permission from the publisher. Checkerboard Library™ is a trademark and logo of Abdo Publishing.

Printed in the United States of America, North Mankato, Minnesota.
052014
092014

THIS BOOK CONTAINS
RECYCLED MATERIALS

Cover Photo: AP Images
Interior Photos: AP Images pp. 1, 5, 7, 9, 11, 13, 17, 22, 23, 25; Corbis pp. 15, 21, 27;
    Getty Images pp. 10, 19, 24, 29

Series Coordinator: Tamara L. Britton
Editors: Megan M. Gunderson, Bridget O'Brien
Art Direction: Neil Klinepier

Library of Congress Cataloging-in-Publication Data
Anderson, Jameson.
  Clay Matthews / Jameson Anderson.
      pages cm. -- (Awesome athletes)
  Includes index.
  ISBN 978-1-62403-334-6
1. Matthews, Clay, 1986---Juvenile literature. 2. Linebackers (Football)--United States--Biography--Juvenile literature. 3. Football players--United States--Biography--Juvenile literature. I. Title.
  GV939.M2964A53 2014
  796.332092--dc23
  [B]
                        2014006376

TABLE OF CONTENTS

MAKING HIS MARK

On October 5, 2009, the rival Green Bay Packers and Minnesota Vikings faced off in Minneapolis, Minnesota. Nearly 64,000 fans filled the Metrodome Stadium. In front of that crowd, Clay Matthews stepped onto the field in his No. 52 uniform. It was his first start as a Packer.

Matthews was at the right outside linebacker position. In the second quarter, Vikings running back Adrian Peterson was plowing his way through Packers. At least, he was until he got close to Matthews. Matthews ripped the football from Peterson's hands.

Matthews quickly realized he had a path to the end zone. He ran the ball back for a touchdown. It was the longest **fumble** return for a touchdown by a **rookie** in Packers history.

Matthews would go on to score defensive touchdowns in the next two seasons as well. He became the first Packers player in history to score a defensive touchdown in his first three seasons.

But being a great football player wasn't always in Matthews's future. It was a long road from being too small to start on his high school team to being a **Super Bowl** champion.

Matthews ran down the right sideline for a 42-yard (38-m) touchdown in his first start as a Packer. The Vikings went on to win 30–23.

HIGHLIGHT REEL

William Clay Matthews III was born in Northridge, California.

1986

Matthews was drafted by the Green Bay Packers with the 26th overall pick.

2009

The Packers won Super Bowl XLV, defeating the Pittsburgh Steelers.

2011

2008

Matthews was named Co-Special Teams Player of the Year for the third year in a row.

2009

Matthews made his first start as a Green Bay Packer.

2012

Matthews was named to his fourth straight Pro Bowl.

CLAY MATTHEWS III

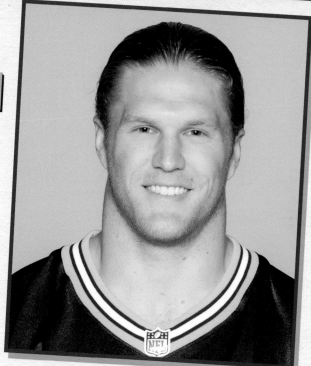

DOB: May 14, 1986
Ht: 6'3"
Wt: 255
Position: OLB
Number: 52

CAREER STATISTICS:

Tackles: 186
Sacks: 50.0
Forced Fumbles: 10

AWARDS:

Co-Special Teams Player of the Year: 2006–2008
Pro Bowl: 2009–2012
Senior Bowl: 2009
Super Bowl Champion: 2011

BORN INTO FOOTBALL

William Clay Matthews III was born on May 14, 1986, in Northridge, California. Clay didn't have a name for the first few days of his life. His parents, Leslie and William Clay Matthews Jr., were expecting him to be a girl. They hadn't picked out names for a son! They finally chose to give him the name his father and grandfather also share.

All his life, Clay has been known by his middle name. He is the second youngest child in a family of five. He has an older sister, Jennifer. His two older brothers are Kyle and Brian. His younger brother is Casey.

The Matthews family is a football family. Clay's grandfather, Clay Matthews Sr., played for the San Francisco 49ers in the 1950s. Clay's father played

FUN FACT CLAY'S UNCLE BRUCE WAS INDUCTED INTO THE NFL HALL OF FAME IN 2007. HE BECAME AN NFL COACH AFTER RETIRING FROM PLAY.

19 seasons for the Cleveland Browns and the Atlanta Falcons, from 1978 to 1996.

Clay's uncle Bruce also played 19 years in the **National Football League (NFL)**, from 1983 to 2001. He played for the Houston Oilers, which became the Tennessee Oilers and then the Tennessee Titans.

Bruce Matthews

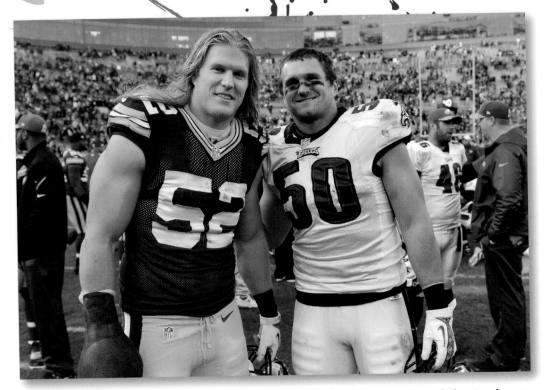

Clay and Casey Matthews met on the field when the Packers played the Eagles on November 10, 2013. Clay played with an injured thumb, and the Packers lost 27–13.

Clay's brother Casey was **drafted** by the Philadelphia Eagles in 2011. Their cousin Jake, Bruce's son, was picked up by the Atlanta Falcons in the 2014 **NFL** Draft.

Clay's grandfather was a defensive end. His uncle was an offensive lineman. Clay took after his father when he became a linebacker. Casey also plays linebacker. Jake is an offensive tackle.

Even though so many men in the Matthews family played football, there was no pressure on Clay or his brothers to play. Clay's father knew that football can be hard on a person's body. He did not want his sons to get injured at an early age.

Clay's parents were careful with him. Before Clay even played football he suffered a head injury. He was knocked unconscious when he fell off his skateboard at just seven years old.

Clay was reckless as a child. His mother said that he wouldn't just dive into the swimming pool at home like most kids would. Instead, Clay liked to jump from the roof of the family's house. He would land on a trampoline and then bounce into the pool!

Jake Matthews was the sixth overall draft pick and the first player drafted from Texas A&M University in 2014.

TAKING HIS TIME

Clay was nine years old before he joined his first youth football league. He lived in Lilburn, Georgia, at the time. But football wasn't Clay's first choice. He signed up because he had missed the sign-up time for soccer!

Eventually, Clay decided that he wanted to be a football player like his father. But still, his father didn't pressure him. Clay said in an interview that his father put more pressure on him to succeed at whatever he tried, on or off the football field.

Clay's family believed in working hard. Even though Clay was the son of a professional football player, he still needed to have a job. So in high school, Clay worked for a moving company. He helped move supplies and equipment when businesses moved offices.

By this time, the Matthews family was back in California. Clay played football and basketball for the Agoura Chargers in Agoura Hills, California. As the

defensive coordinator, Clay's father helped design plays for the football team.

Clay was smaller than other players on the team. He had to be a backup until he grew stronger and gained weight. Clay was 6 feet 1 inch (1 m 85 cm) tall and weighed just 166 pounds (75 kg). Clay's father chose to have stronger players start ahead of Clay. Senior year, Clay grew taller and gained 45 pounds (20 kg). That year, he was finally a starter.

Clay was small in high school. But during college, he bulked up to 6 feet 3 inches (1 m 91 cm) and 240 pounds (109 kg).

COLLEGE HOPEFUL

Because he was small for his age, Clay wasn't sure he would be able to play college football. **Scouts** came to check on high school players. Yet even though Clay came from a football family and worked hard, they weren't interested in him. Scouts look at juniors, and Clay hadn't had his growth spurt yet.

Clay didn't expect to be offered an athletic **scholarship**. When he finally did earn some interest, it was from smaller programs at junior colleges. Clay decided to wait it out and see if any larger universities would notice him and offer him a scholarship.

When none did, Clay **enrolled** at the University of Southern California (USC) in Los Angeles. Clay attended from 2004 to 2008 and **majored** in international relations.

Clay had decided to be a **walk-on**. That meant he was not at USC on a football scholarship, and he had

FUN FACT CLAY'S FATHER, UNCLE, AND BROTHER KYLE ALSO ATTENDED USC.

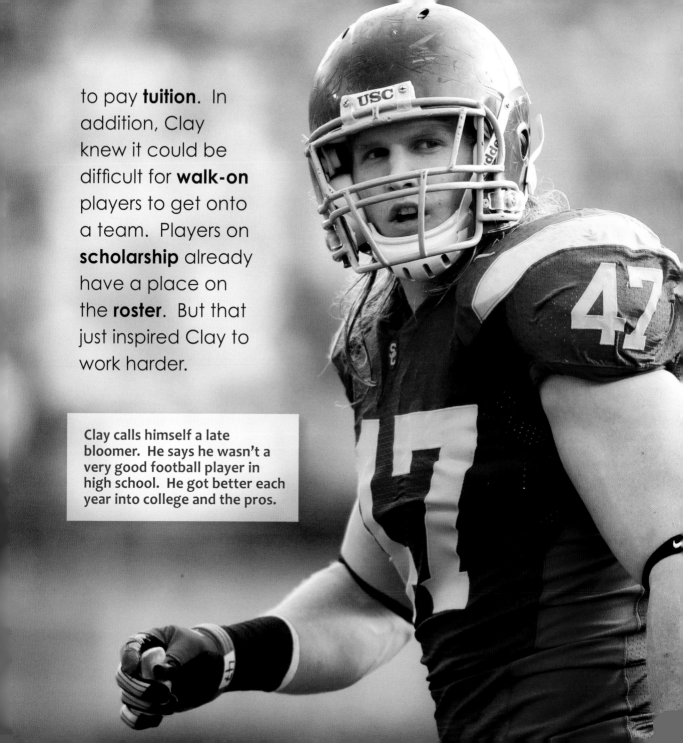

to pay **tuition**. In addition, Clay knew it could be difficult for **walk-on** players to get onto a team. Players on **scholarship** already have a place on the **roster**. But that just inspired Clay to work harder.

Clay calls himself a late bloomer. He says he wasn't a very good football player in high school. He got better each year into college and the pros.

MAKING THE TEAM

Clay didn't play during his first year of college in 2004. He decided to **redshirt** to give himself more time to develop as a player. But that doesn't mean he didn't still prepare for the future. He spent as much time as he could around the football team. Plus, he worked out to get bigger and stronger.

During the 2005 season, Clay became a reserve linebacker. He played defense and on special teams. Clay played 12 of 13 games, missing just one for an elbow injury. He had three tackles against Stanford and two against Washington State. He finished the season with eight tackles, including four solos.

Clay earned a **scholarship** his sophomore season. This time, he played in all 13 games. He recorded 15 tackles, including 4 against Stanford on November 4, 2006. Also at Stanford, he had the first sack of his college career.

FUN FACT TODAY, CLAY IS KNOWN FOR HIS LONG HAIR. GROWING IT OUT STARTED AS A BET WITH OTHER LINEBACKERS IN COLLEGE.

Clay was named USC's Co-Special Teams Player of the Year. He also was honored as a second-team Academic All-Pac 10 Conference selection. In order to be named to an All-Academic team, a college player has to be a starter or a significant substitute player. He also has to have good grades.

Clay sacked Arizona State quarterback Rudy Carpenter on the way to a USC win on October 14, 2006.

PICKING UP STEAM

In 2007, Clay really took off. He played in all 13 games. He started two games, against Nebraska and Washington State. He was an important backup linebacker in the other games. He was also key to the USC Trojans' success on special teams. Clay again was named Co-Special Teams Player of the Year.

Throughout the season, Clay made 17 tackles, 15 solo. That included 4 against Idaho and 3 against Washington State. Clay also blocked two kicks.

But Clay's big moment came in the Rose Bowl. USC played Illinois. Clay made three tackles and forced two **fumbles**. Plus, USC claimed a Rose Bowl-record 633 yards (579 m). The Trojans beat the Fighting Illini 49–17 on national television. Clay was playing on a team some considered the best in college football.

USC led 21–0 in the second quarter of the Rose Bowl. Illinois had a chance in the third to make up the difference, but they could never catch the Trojans.

SENIOR YEAR

Clay was starting to think that he had a future in football. Along with playing, practicing, and working out, Clay also got to know football behind the camera.

Clay was an **intern** at the **NFL** Network. He helped TV announcers prepare before their shows. As an international relations **major** at USC, he had an interest in both football and communications. Clay has said that he might be interested in being behind the camera when his football career is done.

For the 2008 season, Clay began as a reserve but then started his last 10 games as a defensive end. He played in all 13 games and made 56 tackles, 28 solo. He had 9 stops for losses and 4.5 sacks. He also recorded 2 **fumble** recoveries and 2 forced fumbles.

The team again awarded Clay Co-Special Teams Player of the Year. They also honored his work in the weight room with the Co-Lifter of the Year Award.

Clay was seen as a dedicated player on the field and in the weight room. Scouts also admired his burst off the snap. He gets to top speed quickly!

Clay displayed his skills for pro **scouts** at the Senior Bowl, a showcase for college seniors. Unlike during his high school years, Clay's move from college to the **NFL** had the attention of scouts and sports writers. He had played in four straight Rose Bowl games. He had become a star at USC.

The Packers chose wisely in the draft. Matthews became the team's first rookie to be named to the Pro Bowl since 1978.

Matthews wasn't sure which team would take him in the 2009 **NFL Draft**. Some experts didn't think he was good enough to be a first-round pick. Overall, he didn't have as much experience as other available players.

Green Bay Packers general manager Ted Thompson wanted Matthews. So, the Packers traded a second-round pick and two third-round picks to trade up to another first-round slot. They took Matthews with the twenty-sixth overall pick.

Matthews was a critical part of the 2009 Packers season. He had 13 starts in 16 games. The Packers ended their season with the NFC Wild Card game at Arizona.

In the team's high-scoring **playoff** loss to the Cardinals, Matthews started and led the linebackers with seven tackles. The Cardinals beat the Packers 51–45 in **overtime**.

It was tough for the team to get to the playoffs and not make it to the **Super Bowl** championship game. Matthews and his team knew that if they worked hard, they had a strong chance at playing in the Super Bowl the next season.

Matthews recovered two fumbles in the game against Dallas on November 15, 2009. His performance earned him Pepsi NFL Rookie of the Week.

CHAMPIONSHIP SEASON

It only took two seasons with the Packers for Matthews to see his **NFL** dreams come true. The team finished with a 10–6 record, which was second place in the NFC North.

Matthews running for his touchdown against the Cowboys

In the 2010 season, Matthews had 13.5 sacks. He had two 3-sack games in a row early in the season. And, he was the first player in Packers history to record more than 10 sacks in each of his first two years.

There were many other highlights in Matthews's 2010 season. Playing Dallas on November 7, he grabbed a

62-yard (57-m) touchdown. Against the New York Giants on December 26, he had six tackles and a forced **fumble**.

The Packers then stormed through the **playoffs** on their way to **Super Bowl** XLV. With a second-place finish, the team faced the Philadelphia Eagles in the NFC Wild Card game on January 9, 2011. Matthews contributed three solo tackles and four quarterback hits. The Packers won 21–16.

Matthews had 17 sacks in his first 20 games in the NFL.

The Packers then faced the Atlanta Falcons in the NFC Divisional **playoff** game on January 15. Matthews had two sacks, which was a career-first in the playoffs. The Packers won 48–21 on the Falcons' home field.

In the final game before the **Super Bowl**, the Packers defeated the Chicago Bears to win the NFC Championship. Matthews contributed eight tackles. This was another career-high performance in the playoffs. The Packers scored 21 and held the Bears to 14 for the win on January 23.

On February 6, Matthews and the Packers faced the Pittsburgh Steelers in Super Bowl XLV. The game was played at Cowboys Stadium in Texas. Matthews had four tackles and two quarterback hits.

Most important, Matthews had one of the key plays of the game in the fourth quarter. He hit running back Rashard Mendenhall, making him lose his grip on the ball. Linebacker Desmond Bishop recovered it and the Packers scored soon after. After that game-changing forced **fumble**, the Packers won the Super Bowl 31–25.

FUN FACT MATTHEWS'S FAMILY HAS A LONG HISTORY IN THE NFL. BUT, MATTHEWS WAS THE FIRST FAMILY MEMBER TO SEE A SUPER BOWL WIN.

Matthews's forced fumble in the Super Bowl

A BRIGHT FUTURE

The Packers haven't made it back to the **Super Bowl** since after the 2010 season. But Matthews continues to be a team leader. In 2011, the Packers lost just one game in the regular season. Matthews recorded 69 tackles and led the team with six sacks.

In 2012, the Packers lost 45–31 at San Francisco in the Divisional **playoff** game. Matthews missed four games due to injury. But he still had 60 tackles and a forced **fumble**. And, he was named to his fourth straight **Pro Bowl**.

The next season, Matthews contributed three forced fumbles. After a tough season, the Packers lost the wild card game 20–23 to the 49ers.

Winning the Super Bowl and being a strong player brought Matthews the attention of advertisers and other organizations. Because of his long hair, Matthews helps promote shampoo. He has also done ads for athletic gear, phones, and shaving razors.

FUN FACT MATTHEWS'S PLAY-MAKING ABILITIES EARNED HIM THE NICKNAME "THE CLAYMAKER." IN APRIL 2013, THEY ALSO EARNED HIM A FIVE-YEAR, $66 MILLION CONTRACT EXTENSION. THIS MADE HIM THE HIGHEST-PAID NFL LINEBACKER.

Off the field, Matthews works to promote education. He supports the Boys & Girls Clubs of America. He has provided **concussion**-preventing helmets for young players. He also hosts camps for kids who are trying to improve their football skills.

Matthews is glad to pass along his football knowledge to young players. He knows that not everyone is always the right size for football. But Matthews has proven that hard work sometimes means more than size.

Matthews has done TV commercials for products such as Campbell's Soup.

GLOSSARY

concussion - a brain injury caused by a blow to the head.

draft - an event during which sports teams choose new players. Choosing new players is known as drafting them.

enroll - to register, especially in order to attend school.

fumble - to lose hold of a football while handling or running with it.

intern - a student or graduate gaining guided practical experience in a professional field.

major - to study a particular subject or field.

National Football League (NFL) - the highest level of professional football. It is made up of the American Football Conference (AFC) and the National Football Conference (NFC).

overtime - the extra time that is added to a game if the score is tied when the game clock runs out.

playoffs - a series of games that determine which team will win a championship.

Pro Bowl - an all-star game in which the American Football Conference's top players play against the top players from the National Football Conference.

redshirt - to limit a college athlete's participation in a sport for one school year.

rookie - a first-year player in a professional sport.

roster - a list of players on a team.

scholarship - money or aid given to help a student continue his or her studies.

scout - a person who evaluates the talent of amateur athletes to determine if they would have success in the pros.

Super Bowl - the annual National Football League (NFL) championship game. It is played by the winners of the American and National Conferences.

tuition (tuh-WIH-shuhn) - money students pay to receive instruction.

walk-on - a college athlete who tries to play for the school team but has not been specifically recruited.

To learn more about Awesome Athletes, visit **booklinks.abdopublishing.com**. These links are routinely monitored and updated to provide the most current information available.

INDEX